hush

hush

Rosemerry Wahtola Trommer

Middle Creek Publishing & Audio
Beulah, CO
↑

hush
© Rosemerry Wahtola Trommer, 2020

Books may be purchased in quantity and/or special
sales by contacting the publisher. All inquiries related to
such matters should be addressed to:

Middle Creek Publishing & Audio
9167 Pueblo Mountain Park Road
Beulah, CO 81023
editor@middlecreekpublishing.com
(719) 369-9050

First Paperback Edition, 2020
ISBN: 978-1-7332163-7-1

Printed in the United States

Cover Image: Summers Fall, Finn Trommer

Cover Design: David Anthony Martin
Author photo: Real Life Photographs

Contents

A Slender Moment 45

Acknowledgments

I am grateful to the editors of the following journals and books where these poems originally appeared, sometimes in earlier versions:

Clover: "The Field Was High and the Sun Was Low," "Misty"
Deluge: "A Case for Quietude"
Gratefulness: "But You Thought You Knew What a Sign Looked Like"
Encore: "Deciding to Sometimes Practice Being Snapdragon"
Fungi Magazine: "Mushroom Hunting in the Morning"
Inner Forest Service: "Following Mr. Berry's Instructions"
Inspired: Words from the Edge: "I Want to Show You Something"
The Jeff Quartets (composed by Paul Fowler): "First Pink"
Montrose Mirror: "The Blizzard Reminds Me"
Science & Nonduality: "The Thing Is"
Send My Roots Rain: 52 Weeks of Poetry to Heal Your Grief: "No Hurry to Find Out"
Stone Gathering: "Perhaps You Can Hear It," "Swimming to the Island"
Telluride Watch: "One Walk in the Frost"

The Sky Fits on Every Page

I CARRIED THESE POEMS into the desert. Some nights, they went under the back of my head on rock and sand where I slept to the rhythm of her pages. Around a fire, a couple of us read them out loud at the edge of a mesa, stars absurdly numerous, our voices echoing in the canyons below.

I hid them, not intentionally, finding one of Wahtola Trommer's pages folded in a pocket I'd forgotten about days earlier. I opened it and stopped in my tracks as she gave me back my reason for being here. The dream of rain. The smell of juniper. The child of myself being shown the world. She uses the words *fragile* and *persistent* and I can't help becoming aware of my skin and the state of the air. Yes, I say to her poems, I am that fragile and persistent thing. I see where I am on this earth, pushing against it and being folded back.

They are fine for reading indoors, curled up with a cat and rain on the windows, but I believe these kind poems, full of nature, are best carried outside. Their words respond well to wind and the circle of a headlamp. They ask for the back door to close as you walk into the yard, book open in your hands, or to be read at lunch on a bench or tailgate. But inside will do.

I read some of them to my love from the couch, and again at breakfast, first kiss of the day. They are finely scripted love letters, after all. You'd appreciate someone else hearing them. They are sensual. They want to be touched.

The poet's place is dry and wild, with rivers that shrink in the fall. Who else praises drought? The snow she writes about bends the branches of trees you can see with your own eyes. The mountains around her are darkly wooded and there are predators.

Poems don't have to be inside or out. They can be wherever they want, and Wahtola Trommer chooses out. The sky fits on every page. Without closed doors or being bottled up by walls, you can breathe. She wants you to fill your lungs. It feels good. It feels like being outside. Reach your hands into these, get them under your fingernails. Come up looking like you've been rolling in the garden.

— Craig Childs
   Author of Secret Knowledge of Water *and* Virga and Bone

Bowing Our Heads to Move Forward

Clear Night

I ask the night,
teach me to ask bigger questions—
it replies,
perhaps you could
take the pen away
from the one who wants
to ask questions
and then let her come
walk in the night.

Where We Are Headed

At first, we just say flower. How
thrilling it is to name. Then it's
aster. Begonia. Chrysanthemum.

We spend our childhood practicing
how to separate one thing from another.
Daffodil. Edelweiss. Fern. We learn

which have five petals, which have six.
We say, "This is a gladiolus, this, hyacinth."
And we fracture the world into separate

identities. Iris. Jasmine. Lavender.
Divorcing life into singular bits.
And then, when we know how to tell

one thing from another, perhaps
at last we feel the tug to see not
what makes things different, but

what makes things the same. Perhaps
we feel the pleasure that comes
when we start to blur the names—

and once again everything
is flower, and by everything,
I mean everything.

This Very Here

And then came the day
when I knew to stop asking
to be anywhere else,

when somehow I no longer
believed any other garden
was better than this one,

when I wanted only
these weeds and this field.
There will come a day,

I am sure, when I forget.
But today, the freedom
of being utterly tethered

to this very here with no
other dream, no plan
for other plots, just

a song on my lips
that I sometimes
know how to sing

and sometimes
have to hush to hear
how it goes.

Job Description

My work is loving the world.
        —Mary Oliver, "My Work is Loving the World"

My work is to be the student of the buds
that have been on the birch all winter—
tight and red, they know when to clench,
when to wait, when to swell,
when to burst, when to green.

My work is to open like the scent of juniper
when stroked by afternoon sun,
like the gong when rapidly rapped
into a shining explosion of resonance.

And when I am wall, my work
is to add hinges and become door.
And when I am lock, my work
is to find the lost key.

My work is to be baby bird,
to open my beak and take in
whatever the world has to feed me
and then learn to fly.

Lesson from the Trees

Here in the garden
the trees do what trees do—
they do not grow beyond
their ability to support themselves.

In the top of this weeping birch,
the branches are leafless and dead.
They will never grow again,
nor will the tree replace them.

I think of all the ways we try
to heal ourselves, each other.
All the ways we go back to the pain
of the past as if it had some answers.

What if we could let them die,
those thoughts, those wounded ideas
of how it should have been,
let them turn brittle and gray,

and when they have lost their weight,
let them fall away. I see how the breeze
moves through the leaves that remain,
how green they are, how alive.

They Say It's the Best Bloom in Ten Years

She wants to go see the bluebonnets, she says.
This is after she tells me she has three months to live.

And I want to find her vast fields of bluebonnets,
acres and acres of white-tipped blue bloom.

And I want to send her more springs to see them in,
more days to live one day at a time. I want to remove

the pain in her belly, the pain that aggressively grows.
I want to make deals with the universe. Want to say no

to the way things are. I want to tell death to wait.
I want to tell life to find a way. I want to hug her

until she believes she is beloved. I want to give her
the pen that will write every brave thing

that she's been unable to say. There are days
when we feel how uncompromising it is, the truth.

How human we are. There are days when bluebonnets
stretch as far as the eye can see. There are days

we know the most important thing is going to see them,
a billion blue petals all nodding in the wind

teaching us to say yes.

On the Last Day of the World

On the last day of the world, I would want to plant a tree.
        —W. S. Merwin

On the last day of the world, I would want
to feed you. Wild pucker of gooseberries.
Thin slices of apple. Peaches so ripe

they drip down our chins, down our necks.
I would want to sit with you beneath a tree,
no, we'll climb a tree, no, we'll plant a tree,

yes all of these. On the last day of the world,
I want to give myself permission to feel
exactly what I feel, to be exactly who I am,

to shed every layer of should and meet you
that way. Knowing we have only hours left,
could we put down our arguments with ourselves,

each other, and find no energy to pick them up again?
On that day, I want us to write the last poem
together and let the writing undo us, let it teach us

how to get out of the way, how to obey what emerges.
Let's run outside, no matter the weather, and praise
the light till the light is gone, and then praise the dark.

If You Are Lonely

In early October, after the frost,
but before the long white weight of snow,

wade waist-deep in the raspberry thicket,
when the air is cold and the sun is low

and there is yet gold on the mesa's hills,
all glitter and tremble and shine, and hiding

beneath the still green leaves are swollen red berries,
few enough that to find one feels like earning a prize,

but abundant enough to lure you deeper in,
despite the brambles, the snags on your sleeves,

the scratches into your hands. There is no way
to be anywhere but here. The day moves no faster

than shadows can grow and hunger is a thing
that can be sated. The light meets you

exactly where you are and gives itself to you
and asks nothing in return.

Viola papilionacea

And here they are, the wild violets.
How they leap into gardens uninvited,
their tiny purple faces unapologetic, open.
How they thrive amidst the other plants
chosen by the gardener. They do not mind
not being the chosen ones. They thrive.
Tenacity can be so small, so beautiful.

I may not be a powerful woman,
but I have some wild violet in me,
some willingness to insist on renegade beauty,
some desire to be soft and yet persist,
some certainty that the garden
is big enough for us all.

Walking Up the Pass

A mallard swims
in the beaver pond—
the sunlight makes
a green psalm of its head

and for an instant
the whole world
revolves around
emerald sheen.

There is little else
that's green here,
though it is late spring—
but over 10,000 feet

the snow tends to linger.
This is a place where
the mind doesn't hesitate
to offer its attention

to the sharp scent of trees,
to the snaking trickle of snowmelt,
to the thrill of cold air
in the lungs. And in giving

itself away, the mind
becomes clearer, becomes
a shining and natural thing,
like a mallard wing, like

a tree just before leafing,

like a canyon in which
the lush green world
is just about to emerge.

But You Thought You Knew What a Sign Looked Like

Open your hands, lift them.
—William Stafford, "Today"

The parking space beside the store when you
were late. The man who showed up just in time
to hold the door when you were juggling five
big packages. The spider plant that grew—
though you forgot to water it. The new
nest in the tree outside your window. Chime
of distant church bells when you're lonely. Rhyme
of friendship. Apples. Sky a trove of blue.

And who's to say these miracles are less
significant than burning bushes, loaves
and fishes, steps on water. We are blessed
by marvels wearing ordinary clothes—
how easily we're fooled by simple dress—
Oranges. Water. Leaves. Bread. Crows.

No Hurry to Find Out

Joan asks me what happens after we die,
and I don't know, but I do know
how to stand beside the river
and see a shrine in every rock I find,

which is how I spent the day yesterday.
And I know that walking today
in the snow, every step felt like
a prayer, which is to say

I feel so very lucky to be alive,
even though I don't know who
the prayer is to—nor what the point
of praying is—except that on days like today

I overspill with gratitude
and it feels so good to say thank you
for this life that happens before we know
what happens after we die.

Love,

Though I am undeniably broken,
I come to you with no need to be fixed.
I come to you the way one river
meets another river—not joining
out of thirst, but because
there is so much power
and beauty in giving oneself
to another, in moving
through the world together.
I come to you the way the half moon
comes into the yard—I could be more
whole, but in the meantime,
I will bring you everything
I have.

Inner Eden

And if I found in me
a spot of land where
anything could grow—
some miraculous soil
that knows only yes—

then what would
I dare sow?
In such tender
territory, even breath
might take root.

A whisper becomes
a seed becomes
an unknowable
flowering. A song,
of course, I'd plant

a love song.
But imagine if,
as I knelt, lips to earth,
a loneliness spilled
from my pockets,

strewing its millions
of tired spores
throughout the plot.
And what if an arrow
from an old wound

chose then to dislodge?

Oh this dangerous
dance at the edge
of inevitable fertility, longing
for the impossible—

to plant only beauty,
its fruits reseeding
all around us growing
only more beauty,
more beauty.

Walking Up the Mill Creek Road,
Practicing How to Be Alive

You could leave life right now. Let that determine what
you do and say and think.
    —Marcus Aurelius, Meditations

And though the leaves blush golden and red
and though the sun cups my face like a hand
and though the chill air makes me catch my breath

the wind whispers, *friend, remember your death.*
And I feel so deeply, so wildly alive
as I climb the hill, slight burn in my thighs

but I cannot pretend I am deaf
as the wind whispers soft, *remember your death.*
The Roman generals had their slaves

whisper to them in their moments of greatness,
remember your death—even as the crowds cheered—
to help them remember *be humble, be here.*

And the wind whispers *yes,* whispers *yes* to me.
And reminds me to move forward gratefully.
Remember your death, it says. *Live now.*

So I thrill in the evergreen trees—even now
they spike the air with their sharp green scent—
and each step, each step, I remember my death.

After Reading "What's in the Temple" by Tom Barrett, I Consider His Question

If you had a temple in the secret spaces of your heart,
what would you worship there?
What would you bring to sacrifice?
What would be behind the curtain in the holy of holies?
     —Tom Barrett, "What's in the Temple"

In the secret temple of my heart
was an altar with nothing on it—
I love nothing, the pure potential
of it. Sometimes when others
journeyed there, I sensed
they were surprised,
perhaps even sorry for me,
as if the altar would be better
with a lotus or a cross
or a star or a figurine
or a photo of someone.
Or a stone. Always something.

I tried, in fact, to put things
on the altar, but no thing let itself stay.

There was a day
when, in a single moment,
the altar had *everything*
on it—every bee, every stick,
every plastic bag, beetle,
every crushed empty can,
every crumpled shirt,
every door handle, compass,

broken thermometer, apple,
trash can, tree, *everything*.

Then, the altar was no longer
in some secret temple in my heart,
but everywhere. Everywhere
a place to worship. Everything a prayer
waiting to be heard, to be touched.
What is not held and infused
by the holy? Even nothing. Even these eyes.
Even these tears.

Good Morning, Destiny

And what isn't a sign this morning—
the way the alarm lost its ring,

the scent of apples waiting to be peeled,
the blue reveal behind morning mist,

a green street sign that reads Paradise,
the mountains themselves moving

until it appears the sun rises.
Everything feels worthy

of attention, of notice. We need
not scour for omens. What

doesn't have something to say
to us about where we are going:

five black crows on the fence line,
a missing glove, the trees shedding

whatever no longer serves them,
the sun so bright in our eyes

we must bow our heads
to move forward.

Misty

And sometimes when I move
at the edge of a greatness—
a lake or a sea or a mountainside—

my insignificance thrills me
and the largest of my sadnesses
dwindles smaller than the space

between grains of sand
and in that moment,
knowing my place,

comes a love so enormous
I can love anyone, anyone,
even myself.

Thigmomorphogenesis and Other Sweet Nothings

This, too, is love, the way the beans
reach for the fence, the way the fence
does not leave the garden. The way
plants long to be touched—how
it keeps them from growing spindly
and weak. How the spider plant
on the shelf drops tiny white petals
into the cups. You could say it's just
nature doing what nature does.

I prefer to call it love, the sunflowers
nodding their brown faces east every
morning, the lilies of the valley
spreading their generous perfume.

Perhaps You Can Hear It?

Whatever an open field has always tried to say,
that's what I long to say to you. That, and the blue thrill
that trills in the larkspur just before it blooms.

And the communion of threads in the blanket,
the sincerity of wild strawberries, and
whatever it is that lavender says to the nose—

those are the notes I would write into the song
I'm still learning to sing, this song I would tuck
into your back pocket so that you might,

in the middle of a day, perhaps, find it there,
like stars behind the blue noon sky
just waiting to appear.

Ode to Tears

The way day doesn't fight
the dim before night. The way
shore does not resist the river's rise.
The way air does not refuse
the beat of wing—that's the way
I want to let tears come.
Why do I try to force
them from falling?
Not that it works anyway.
Still, this defiance, this struggle
to appear unmoved. And why?
When there are children who laugh
and a sky that blues and stories
that break us and laughter that
seizes us? Why try to pretend
we are not changed by the way
a child loves her mother or
a friend perseveres through cancer
or the way a math teacher reminds us we have
86,400 seconds a day to spend
and if we don't spend them,
they are gone. It is logical to weep
when met with beauty, it is practical
to let the tears release instead
of all this stupid pretending that
we are too cool or too smart or too
sophisticated to be stirred.
No, better to notice when our toes
are dipped in the grand stream
that unites us all and let that water
move right through our eyes—

better not to try to explain it.
Better to wade in the course of tears
and refuse any boat that would keep us
from touching the water. After all,
we know how to swim. After all,
there are so many reasons
to give in to who we are.

And Again

And what if I never get it right,
this loving, this giving of the self
to the other? And what if I die

before learning how to offer
my everything? What if, though
I say I want this generous,

indefatigable love, what if
I forever find a way to hold
some corner back? I don't want

to find out the answer
to that. I want to be the sun
that gives and gives until it burns out,

the sea that kisses the shore
and only moves away so that
it might rush up to kiss it again.

Big

This is, perhaps, the year to learn to be big.
Spruce tree big. Cliffside big. Big as mesa,
as mountain lake. Big as in cosmos, as in love.
Being small has never served me—constricting,
contorting, trying to fit into a room, into shoes,
into a name. Let this be the year to escape all those little
rules with those little shoulds, all those little
cages with their little locks. Time to make of myself
a key, time to lean into immensity. Time to supersize
communion, time to grow beyond self. Time to
open, to unwall, to do as the universe does,
accelerating as I expand, not rushing toward
something else, no, but changing the scale
of space itself.

A Slender Moment

Beside the Lake, A Note to Self

If you watch the heron as it stalks
amongst the tall green reeds, then pauses,
and in its pausing disappears, then you understand
something of the power of stillness.

And if you sit still long enough
to see the head of the snapping turtle
rise between the lily pads,
then you glean something of the rewards
that come with sitting still.

But if you sit expecting such rewards,
then perhaps sit longer and watch the cattails
as they waver and still, sway and still and still,
and feel how the urge in you to say something rises
and softens and softens until there is nothing to say,

until that kind of stillness becomes
the greatest reward, until you feel
stillness hold you the way the lake
holds the lily pad, the way silence holds a song,
the way gratitude holds everything.

Raking the Leaves with Jack

Pulling the rake through the cottonwood leaves,
I think of Jack in Michigan pulling his rake

through beech, birch, oak and ash leaves.
I stop to lean on my rake and I think

of him stopping to lean on his rake
and talk to the gods. I'm not so sure I believe

in gods, but I believe in Jack. I believe in kindness.
I believe in friendship that grows despite distance.

I believe that these rhythms of raking and making piles
bring us closer together—all of us rakers, all of us

who step into the slow cadence of pull and reach,
and pull and reach. There is something unifying

in this annual act of tidying the world. Every day
the news is full of all we can't set right. But we

can drag the rake through the yard so that we
can see the path again. And we can set the rake

aside and stare at the sky and think of all
the people we love and all the people

we'll never know who join us in this simple act,
reach and pull, reach and pull, reach and pull,

the sound of metal tines grating, the beat
of our own hearts scraping against our chests.

Following Mr. Berry's Instructions

You have to be able to imagine lives that aren't yours.
—Wendell Berry

And so today I'm the cottonwood
in the yard, the one we planted twenty years ago,
the one my son used to climb,
the one that we hang bird feeders from, and piñatas,
the one that even now is losing its leaves,
and I imagine standing there year after year,
fall after fall, now after endless now.

What is now for a tree? How different
is now from infinity? I imagine being
my own soaring cathedral, my roots
always thirsting, my wood growing
to seal my wounds, my branches
always chasing the light.

Concentric

See, I want to say to my son. See
how the pond has frozen in thick,

continuous curves. See all the lines,
how they ring each other, like dozens

of tiny orbits. I want to show him
the marvel of it all, but he is too old

now for marvels, or perhaps too young,
the precise age where beauty is boring.

So I take the child of myself to the pond
and show her the rings. I resist the urge

to explain how they were formed by meltwater
and surface tension forces. Instead,

I let her gaze at the miracle,
trace the concentric bands with her fingers.

How curious the rings are, like frozen halos
that fit enormous angels. How astonishing

in their design. Just wait till I show her
we can walk on it, too.

I let her amazement
become my own, our feet slipping

across the smooth surface, our breath
rising in white ephemeral curls.

One Walk in the Forest

seven degrees—
even the barbed wire fence
wears diamonds

Swimming to the Island

I didn't intend to swim to the island.
Told myself it was just a quick slip
into the water. Told myself I would
rejoin the others soon. But the water
said yes to me. And my arms and legs
seemed to remember then
exactly what they were made for.
Sometimes we're in service to something
more primal, a voice that says *go, go,*
keep going, though there's no race,
no finish line, no prize, no spectators,
nothing but the thrill of becoming
the body's bright verb. Feel how
the water buoys you, even as your weight
pulls you down, how it shimmers as far as
a woman can swim, how with each
stroke of your dripping arms,
the lake christens you again and again
a child of this here, this now.

Yes, That's When

I like my body when I'm in the woods
and I forget my body. I forget that arms,
that legs, that nose. I forget that waist,

that nerve, that skin. And I aspen. I mountain.
I river. I stone. I leaf. I path. I flower.
I like when I evergreen, current and berry.

I like when I mushroom, avalanche, cliff.
And everything is yes then, and everything
new: wild iris, duff, waterfall, dew.

Communion

At midday, I dug beneath damp straw
and gently ran my fingers through dirt,
and, there, in the kingdom of earthworms,
found dozens of beautiful ruby-skinned potatoes,
each one of them precious in my hands.

God knows I have longed to be found this way—
pulled out from my darkness and cradled,
held up to the light with an oooh and an ahhh
and a laugh of joy, though I'm slightly misshapen,
though I'm bumpy and imperfect.

There are days when I see through it so easily,
the longing to be loved, and I simply feel the love
that always exists, the love that grows in darkness,
that is utterly unconcerned with worthiness,
that feels no need for discovery.

There are moments when I can't imagine
I ever thought I was lost, like today,
kneeling in the dirt, marveling at the beauty
of potatoes, mud-smudged and lumpy,
knowing myself as another who belongs to the earth.

The Blessing

Sometimes I forget
the trees. It's embarrassing
to admit. Like saying I forget

I have hands. But
days go by when I do not
consider them. And then

some mornings, today,
for instance, the trees,
like an Indian saint

hurling petals at her attendants,
throw their fluffy white catkins
into my hands, my hair,

into my everywhere. I look
until everything is baptized
in white cotton down

and I half expect the giant limbs
to pull me into a great gray trunk
and hold me close, whispering

into my ear, in words so quiet
no one else can hear, my daughter,
my daughter, my daughter, my daughter.

The Field Was High and the Sun Was Low

*after Wallace Stevens, "The House Was Quiet and the
World Was Calm"*

The field was high and the sun was low
and the woman became the light; and the evening

slowed its pace, perhaps to let the light remain.
The field was high and the sun was low.

She moved as though there were no night
worth fearing, as if the field could hold it all.

She leaned into the goldening, the way
the light itself leans softly on the world.

The night, a gentle friend, meandered quietly
across the land. There were no words

that could be said. The field was high
and the sun was lower. Slowly, hushed,

the wind a sigh, the field surrendered
all its lines. The darkness gathered

everything, the field, the woman, even
light, and made itself an offering.

Encouragement

Some mornings, when the sun
has just begun to slip
into my room, I swear

that it encourages me
as I try to hide beneath the sheets.
You can do it, the light seems to say.

It does not mention, not even once,
all the darkness it has traveled through
just to arrive at this window

so that it might warm my face
and suggest there is so much
more light to be found.

Deciding to Sometimes Practice Being Snapdragon

All morning, I make myself useful—
mow the lawn and vacuum
the carpet and scrub the potatoes
and slice the melon and straighten
the shelves and look out the window
and see the snapdragons I planted
last spring not because they were useful,
but because they are so beautiful.

I've Heard It in the Chillest Land

Already the frost has come,
both intricate and merciless,
and it has taken the basil,

the green beans, the zinnias
and whatever hope we had
that summer might never end.

We knew our hope was irrational,
but that's never stopped a hope before.
Every day there's more evidence

against hope—the headlines,
the angry boy down the street,
the child bride in Afghanistan.

And still it rises up, slightly
browned, but still shining
like that marigold bloom that was hiding

beneath a sunflower leaf—
it should be frosted and dead, but
it's not. Damn hope. Never

acting the way we think it will.
May it trick us forever into choosing
to live another day. And after a long winter

when we're sure it's gone, may it always
reseed, putting up dozens of green starts.
Oh brazen hope, oh stubborn hope, oh hope.

I Want to Show You Something, He Said as We Stood in the Library Halls in Boulder, Utah

The candle is not there to illuminate itself.
  —*Nawab Jan-Fishan Khan,* The Way of the Sufi

It will only take five minutes, he said,
and so, though I'd not spoken with him before
and though I was about to teach a class,
I followed him outside the library door
to the dirt lot where his truck was parked
and from the open pick up bed
he pulled with flourish a rolled-up rug
and spread it between the rabbit brush
and milk thistle, then hoisted
two flat wooden seats he'd fashioned
out of pine, arranged them on the rug,
and swung a bench-like table from the bed
and placed it in the center.

And I expected, what, well, not
what happened next. It's your canoe,
he said, and from his truck he plucked
a long and knobby stick. And here's your oar,
he offered, with a slight bow of his head.
I took it up and kicked my shoes off, stepped
onto the rug, then leapt up on the table top
and began to paddle the air.

Where are we going then, I said,
my eyes on the horizon.
To Java, he said, and I paddled harder,
eager to reach its shores. I've always

62

wanted to go to Java, I said, pulling
through currents of air. And look,
he said, there's a farmer there on the banks
saying his morning prayers.
And he pulled from the truck a large
straw hat that he set upon his head
and a simple white scarf he let
slip through his fingers in a ritual
of silk. And when my boat came near,
he stepped beside it, met me
with a bowl-shaped bell, and circled
the small canoe, baptizing the air
with its one-note song. I closed my eyes,
and felt the tone open inside me,

and when I let my lids fly up,
he was standing right in front of me
with a vial of dark oil that smelled of vanilla
and evergreen. And he anointed me,
touching the oil to my head with his finger.
I knew I had arrived. I jumped down and hugged
the farmer, then searched the ground
for a smooth white stone to give him in return.

And as I journeyed back to the library,
somehow now only steps away, I took with me
the scent of pine, the smile of the native man,
the joy that comes when all the lines
we thought we knew have been erased,
and our inner map wildly rearranged.

Reverie

In the pond, it is easy to let go of the paddle,
to let the wind move my little boat
wherever it will. I feel no need to change direction,
no sense that one way is better than another,
no attachment to arriving on any shore.

Dragonflies skim bluely above the water.
Cotton drifts through the air like midsummer snow.
Robins sing their simple song. In this moment,
somehow unstitched from the calendar,
everything seems possible—like a woman

who feared she could not love could do so.
And a day could open in surprising ways,
new worlds spilling into this familiar world.
And a chapter could be written inside another
so that we would never, ever get to the end.

Busy Girl's Satori

Across the yard, below
the cliffs, and just beneath
the evening's drift toward

darkening, above the river,
through the trees,
there is, if you are lucky,

a slender moment charmed
by chance when, if you look up,
the great blue heron

will angle past on slanting wing
and make you question
everything.

With Any Luck

Meet me in summer
when the mountains
are softened by fields

of blue lupine
and the creeks run clear
with the memory of snow.

With any luck,
we'll get lost until
we, too, begin to bloom,

until whatever is cold in us
melts and races away
with a bright and bubbling laugh.

There are days we forget
how to make a fist,
how to speak any language

but praise. Meet me
in summer when the old
high trails are open—

what else might we find
behind the crumbling
mines—some share

of ourselves we've yet
to meet—something
so spacious we never

dreamt it would fit
inside our skin. With any luck,
it will follow us home.

But It's Not the Same

Beside the moss
beside red rock

we walk, we walk
to the falls and talk

and long, long after
you have gone,

the empty space
you left near me

walks on with me,
walks on.

A Case for Quietude

Arriving at the starting line
I think of the marathon to come—
somewhere there's a man

with a gun and a timer.
Somewhere there's another line
I hope to cross.

Somewhere there's a woman
who doesn't know there is a race.
She knows only that the juncos

have come, and if she is still enough
she can see their white tail feathers
flashing in flight.

Never Mind It Was a Dream

because when the wise old man said
that the loving itself
was all that mattered—
somehow, for that moment,
while his suggestion still hung
like perfume in the air,
all the stubborn queries
of how and why and when
that usually knock and crack
and rap and ring, they all lay down
to take a nap,
and in that fragrant silence,
what rose was the most
audacious tenderness,
a shining faith,
how improbably it opened
like a stone turned iris,
like a bone blooming
into spring.

Yes

It's Saturday and I'm choosing to sit on a broken fence,
the logs all weathered and fallen.
I am choosing to sit in the sun on a broken fence
beside a dirt parking lot in a high desert.
Perhaps I do not really believe
that this is the only moment that matters?
Perhaps I don't trust that I could be gone,
that all life could be gone in one blink,
in one bomb, in one meteorite.

Or is it that I choose to sit on a broken fence
beside a dirt parking lot with the scent of pine
edging each breath and the sound
of cottonwood leaves rustling then stilling
because this, too, matters, this willingness
to treat each breath as if it were the first,
to treat each place as if it is the last
and give it my full attention. To be like the birds
sitting on the barbed wire knowing now, now
is the moment to sing.

Despite the Unleafing

That time of year thou mayst in me behold .... Bare ruined
choirs, where late the sweet birds sang.
　　　—William Shakespeare, "Sonnet 73"

And though the leaves may fall and molder,
though the winter nights get colder,
and though, my love, we both grow older,
may the choir in me that sings for you
be ever clear and ever blue—
the stream beneath your red canoe.

And though it seems that time's a thief
and leaf subsides to crumbled leaf
and though the days are gnawed by grief,
may I sing for you forever sweet
in tunes both tame and indiscreet—
sing bare, unruined, my heart, my beat.

Walking at Night

One way to open your eyes to unnoticed beauty is to ask yourself, "What if I had never seen this before? What if I knew I would never see it again?"
        —Rachel Carson, The Sense of Wonder

And so I memorize how it is
that the cheeks nearly freeze,
but the body's so warm,
how the river informs every measure,
but the thoughts sift to silence,
how the body thrills
in its ability to swing one foot
in front of the other, how
walking is just another name
for recovering from falling,
how strange it seems now
that I was once afraid of the dark.

Shavasana

Once again, the field rehearses how to die.
Some of the grass turns golden first. Some
simply fades into brown. Just this morning,

I, too, lay in corpse pose, practicing
how to let myself be totally held by the earth
without striving, how to meet the day

without rushing off to do the next necessary
or beautiful thing. Soon, the grass will bend
or break, molder or disintegrate. Every year,

the same lesson in how to join
the darkness, how to be unmade, how quietly
we might lean into the uncertainty,

how generous the ground.

Turning Each Obstacle into Song

What the Path Thinks

Tonight the path
is tired of being
a path, would rather

be a leaf. Enough
with being beaten.
Enough with leading

the way. Rather to bud,
to unfurl, to serve,
to let go, to get lost.

Really, how hard could it be?
Something about "path"
suggests certainty.

The path feels like a fraud.
It's exhausted with arrivals.
It wants to fall off.

It wants to cartwheel
across the field
like last year's leaves,

to be blown in April wind.
It wants to have no idea
at all where it is going.

There Is Only the Field

We stand in the field.
I swallow any words
that might try to fix things.
Some things cannot be fixed.
Instead, we say the words
that make us weep.
Grief stands with us then,
and holds us
with unforeseen gentleness,
its arms impossibly kind.
It starts to rain.
We do not move to leave.

The Berry Bush

I knew that they were poisonous, the berries.
Still, I used them to make soup. They were
the most beautiful shades of yellow, green
and orange, and they popped when you squeezed them
and spilled their sticky juice, their tiny seeds.
I'd stir them into puddle water with handfuls
of ripped green grass, small stones, broken sticks.
Then I'd stir. Stir and chant into the old silver pot,
chant words I imagined had been sung long before.
It was a soup, I knew, that could heal.
A magical soup that could nourish the world
just in the making of it.

Years later I consider what I knew then—
how belief is the most important ingredient.
How all healing begins with a bit of poison.

Example

Above my window
two tiny hummingbird beaks
peek out just beyond the edge of a nest
which is smaller than my hand—
by fall, they will be in Mexico.
They don't even know yet
they can fly.

How to Unshovel the Snow, An Evening Conundrum

It's not so much that you want the snow
back in the drive, it's just that your back
felt so much better before the shoveling,

and so, using your sideways logic, you think
to yourself that if the snow were unshoveled
your back might unhurt. And while

you're at it, you think you might unthink
those thoughts you thought the night before
shoveling the drive. Though they didn't

amount to any action, now that you've
thought them they've become a frame
that's changed everything. So you start

with the snow, because revising that seems easier
than anything else, but to shovel it back
in the drive would seem to exacerbate

the problem with the back, so
you consider ways the snow might unfall,
all of them fanciful. At least for a while,

it amuses you, the idea of ten million
million snowflakes rising, but then
the reality of drought returns and you

feel guilty for unwishing the snow. No,
better to put your hope in perseverance,
better to put your hope in healing.

It happens. And you walk up the drive,
so snowless and clear you can safely look up
at the sky and see all those stars. The snow

gathers whatever light there is. It can't
unshine. You thrill a bit in the chill. Some
of the shine reaches into you. Some of it stays.

Challenge Lover's Prayer

And let there be rain,
though the path is easier
when dry, and let there be
a bend in the road.
Let us think we know
where we are going—
and let us be wrong.
There are wings in us
we've forgotten.
Let us walk until
we remember them.
And then, let us walk
for the joy of walking.
Because the clapping sound
as our feet meet the earth.
Because puddles.

First Pink

In the loss
     is a branch
     with a brittle
     stem
     where an old
     fruit hangs
     rust-colored
     and dried
     beside
     a tight cluster
     of rose-tipped buds
     where something
     fragile
     and persistent
     is just
     beginning
     to open.

Unlikely Love Song

Praise the summer, its endless drought.
How we'd rather revile it,
change it, would rather pray

for the world to be another way.
Let's chant hymns for the sky, its relentless blue,
and the dry field that crunches

beneath our feet.
We dream of green, dream
of laughing in the rain, dream

of puddles and the thin river
rising. But praise the scarcity,
how it teaches us what

we would rather not know—
how fragile the balance,
how everything matters,

how through struggle we grow.

One More Chapter in Letting Go

Today it slipped into my daughter,
the seed that all is not right in the world.

In a matter of hours, already
the tap roots had grown beyond

my ability to pull them out.
I wonder if I have been wrong

to keep her garden so tidy.
I wonder how to best teach her

to tend her own rows.
It will be endless now,

the onslaught, as every gardener knows.
And there is some pleasure in tending.

I think of how I would rather
be aware of all that grows.

I think of how sometimes
we change our minds

about what is wanted
and what is a weed.

Some part of me longs
to swing the sun back to yesterday.

Some part of me rejoices
that now all the world is her garden.

Wish

And when at last
the healing comes,

may it come like the rain
after a long drought,

so soft that at first
you aren't sure

it is raining,
but the fragrance

overcomes you,
green and wet,

and the world
looks dewy and

you feel it in your lungs.
Yes, may the healing

arrive on the edge
of perception

and then feel
wholly present,

as today when the rain turned
long and steady,

the kind that slowly
saturates and changes everything

so quietly that
you almost don't remember

what it was like before
and everywhere you look,

all you see is shining.

Eventually

Not until the darkness came
did I hear the river, the insistent

clear of it. All the bright day
I had listened to the ding

of the timer, the ring of the phone,
the whine of the boy and the sob

of the girl, the scrabble of kittens,
the turn of engines, the click

of my shoes, the printer's gray hum.
And then, once the dishes were done

and the boy was asleep and
the girl was asleep and the phone

was off and the lights
were out and I lay in the patient

dark, I heard it, the changing flush
of the river's rush, which surely

had been there all day, the river
doing what a river does—flowing

over whatever stands in its path
and turning each obstacle into song.

When I Thought I Wanted Things to Be Different

Sometimes, she said, being uncomfortable
is what we need to do.

And I think of the scald of hot water,
how it cleans the stain.

How being covered in abrasive fuzz
is the only way to harvest the peach.

How the seed is carried by the burr.
It is human to seek pleasure, shun pain.

But think of the tree, how it lets
the gale rip away what is dead.

And the grape, how it bubbles
and foams before it becomes wine.

And the cactus, how it needs the drought
as much as it needs the rain.

Mushroom Hunting in the Morning

Just as you give up,
there, through the trees,
you see a clearing
and though it's exhausting
to be hopeful again
when there's so little
to show for your hope,
you walk to the clearing
and there in the moss,
hundreds of chanterelles.

When you leave
to reenter the broken world,
some of the hope
sticks to you like tiny burrs,
able to seed themselves
anywhere you carry them.
By noon, nearly everything
seems possible.

The Thorn Bush Speaks

You think it's so much better to be petal,
pink flower, the perfumed bloom that lures

the bee. You with your flutter and blush.
Not all of us can be soft. Not all of us

can be beauty, and you have that role
all wrapped up. You with your tender buds,

your loveliness splayed. But I was not
made that way. Was made prick. Was

made barbed. Was made snappish
and piercing and sharp. Was made

fierce. Was made lance. Was made
to take no chances with survival.

There is glory in defense. Everything
that touches me remembers. I'm the one

that defines the scene. How would you know
your beauty without me?

Especially When It Seems Impossible

Try to praise the mutilated world.
        —Adam Zagajewski, "Try to Praise the
        Mutilated World"

The cratered earth
and the blood-stained shirts
and the men with guns
and the hate sharp words
and the sour rooms
that never see sun
and the rashes, the cancers
the blackened lungs

and still, there are paths
in Ohio woods
where upended trees
show elaborate roots
and the water seeps
in the ancient gorge,
and dead leaves fuel
whole dominions of soil

and though beauty
can be hard to reconcile,
worse to ignore it,
worse to look away,
worse in this mutilated world
to pretend we don't have
ten thousand times ten thousand
reasons to praise.

As Winter Remembers Itself

Despite the wind with its whipping twists
and the sting of the fierce face slaps of snow,

the day invites us to enter, to go lightly
into its rumpled hills—though the path

is erased by drifts, though we fall and struggle
to stand again. Sometimes the call

to fall in love with the day is easier to hear
when it's hardest to imagine how.

Bitter gusts and swirling gusts
and gusts that steal our words.

Trying to fall in love never works.
It is more a matter of getting out

of our own way—not trying to orchestrate
the storm, just finding a way to play in it.

Heavy snow. Dim snow. The sky rushes
to fill in the tracks where we've been.

There are no tracks for where we are going.
There is this call to fall deeper in.

Autumn Beside the River

The rocks that were underwater
two months ago are dry now,
and a woman can sit on them
beneath the bridge and escape
the September sun. But she can't
escape herself. There was a time
she really believed she could control things.
Now she sits with her own brokenness
and invites the inevitable autumn into her,
the autumn that's already come.
Invites the lengthening nights. Invites
the dank scent of the garden, moldering and dead.
Invites the loss of green. *You can't be
a sapling forever*, she tells herself,
though another part of her argues,
Yes, you can, yes, you can.

The river has never been so clear—
every rock in the bed is visible now,
and perhaps clarity is one of autumn's best gifts.
She imagines the leaves of her falling off—
how she loves them.
She imagines them golden in the wind.

Just When You Think It's Over:
A Kind of Grammar Lesson

I'm now going to dazzle myself with the pluperfect.
      —Jack Ridl

And isn't it dazzling, the notion
that an action not only began in the past,

but was finished in the past, or,
as they say in Latin, it was perfect.

Not like these leaves, that began
in the past as green flags, but now

transform into gold flame. And we all know
what happens next. No, it's not like

the boy who once fit in my lap
and now looks me in the eye.

Not like the dream I once had for my life
that changed before it could

be achieved. What really ends?
What do our cells not remember?

Even the dead are here in this room,
on the streets, in cafes. We carry

our history with us everywhere
we go, and it wriggles out of its

perfect cage and dances through the ending,
though we thought we'd shut the curtain,

though the director has long since yelled "cut,"
though the audience has already left,

see, here it is, even now, progressive
and as present as these cut sunflowers,

spilling their pollen all over the table,
hardening their seeds into tomorrow's gold.

Directions

It is not that the path
has disappeared. It is only
that, stunned with grief
and kicked by fear,
we sometimes lose our will
to put one foot
in front of the other.
But we are not lost.
Already in the dark
we have found each other.
What astonishes is
that there are so many of us,
and already with our voices
we are building bridges
made of light.
The world shakes,
we stumble
and we help each other rise,
and now it is time
for us again to put one foot
in front of the other—
not to escape what frightens us
but to walk unflinchingly
toward the messy center of things.
The path we choose now
is not one we've walked
or even seen before,
the path is one that appears
beneath our feet
with each step,
and we persist,

travelers in the frozen dark
who begin to see the light
as it shapes the horizon
and know, though it's cold,
that the change we dream of
has already begun to arrive.

The Thing Is

after Ellen Bass's poem by the same name

To trust life, that is the thing.
To trust it even when there are gaping holes
in the walls of your certainty.

To trust it even when your foundation
feels like a strange place filled with strange people
who all feel more at home in you than you do.

And when fear enters you like a bear in your basement,
or like three bears, all of them famished,
all of them rummaging through your emergency stores,

yes, when fear offers to give you its name,
when fear brings you a ladder and says, Here,
climb down into yourself, into this chamber

of strangers and bears,
when you would rather go anywhere but in,
that is when you step onto the rungs and go down,

one rung at a time. No gun in your hand.
No bear spray. No knife. There is honey
in here somewhere. And tea. So much here

to offer these hungriest parts of yourself.
And you are ready to make peace.
You are ready to meet them and share.

I'm Not Saying We Shouldn't Be Angry

I'm not saying we shouldn't be angry.
Anger seems reasonable. But perhaps
we will do what I've heard the Inuit do—

spend the emotion on walking, walk a line
until all the anger has left our bodies.
The moment the Inuit notice the anger is gone,

replaced, perhaps, by sadness or fear,
compassion or just a quietness,
they mark that spot with an object

to show the extent of their anger.
And perhaps, if we're lucky, when we walk
this way, it will be a long enough walk

that we arrive at each other's doors,
object in hand, and when the object
leaves our grip, we'll be able to use our hands

to greet each other, touch each other's faces,
point to the horizon and all the other places
we might choose to walk now together.

The Blizzard Reminds Me

The way the spruce tree
holds the wet snow—how

in a blizzard its branches
will bend and bend

and bend until they release—
that is the way I want to love you,

want to trust that I can hold
the weight of you as you fall,

as you continue to fall,
hold you until it seems I will break

and then, just when I'm sure
I can't take any more,

release you back into yourself—
not in anger, not in fear,

not with guilt—release you
with green resilience

so that come the next storm
I am prepared

to catch you again, again,
and let you go.

How It Might Happen

The baby black swift is born behind a waterfall.
It never leaves its nest until one autumn day
it leaves the damp familiar and starts to fly.

Though it has never flown before, it will not land
until it reaches Brazil, thousands of miles away.

There is, perhaps, a wing inside forgiveness.
Just because it has never flown before,
just because it's never seen beyond the watery veil
does not mean that it won't instantly learn
what it can do.

Like the baby black swift, forgiveness has no idea
what it's flying toward. It only knows
that it must fly and not stop until it is time to stop.

It sounds so miraculous, audaciously impossible.

It is not a matter of courage. It is simply
what rises up to be done, the urge to follow
some inaudible call that says *now, now.*

p. 20: "Job Description" epigraph is from "Messenger" by Mary Oliver, from *Thirst* (Beacon Press, 2006)

p. 23: "On the Last Day of the World" epigraph is from W.S. Merwin on the home page of merwinconservancy.org

p. 28: "But You Thought You Knew What a Sign Looked Like" epigraph is from "Today" by William Stafford, from *My Name is William Tell: Poems* (Confluence Press, 1992)

p. 33: "Walking Up the Mill Creek Road, Practicing How to Be Alive" epigraph is from *Meditations: A New Translation* by Marcus Aurelius and translated by Gregory Hays (Modern Library, 2003)

p. 34: "After Reading "What's in the Temple" by Tom Barrett, I Consider His Question" epigraph is from "What's In the Temple" by Tom Barrett, from *Poetry of Presence: An Anthology of Mindfulness Poems,* edited by Phyllis Cole-Dai and Ruby R. Wilson (Grayson Books, 2017)

p. 55: "Yes, That's When" has a partial first line from e.e. cummings, "I like my body," from Complete Poems 1904-1962 (Liveright Publishing, 1991)

p. 50: "Following Mr. Berry's Instructions" epigraph is from *Wendell Berry* by Morris Allen Grubbs (2007).

"Conversations with Wendell Berry", p.177, University Press of Mississippi

p. 61: "I've Heard It in the Chillest Land" title is a line from "Hope is the thing with feathers (314) by Emily Dickinson, public domain

p. 62: "I Want to Show You Something, He Said as We Stood in the Library Halls in Boulder Utah" epigraph is a quote from Nawab Jan-Fishan Khan in *The Way of the Sufi* by Idries Shah (ISF Publishing, 2015)

p. 71: "Yes" epigraph is from "Yes," by William Stafford, found in The Way It Is: New and Selected Poems (Graywolf Press, 1998)

p. 72: "Despite the Unleafing" epigraph is from "Sonnet 73" by William Shakespeare, public domain

p. 73: "Walking at Night" epigraph is from *The Sense of Wonder* by Rachel Carson (Open Road Media, 2011)

p. 96: "Especially When It Seems Impossible" epigraph is from "Try to Praise the Mutilated World" by Adam Zagajewski, found in *Without End: New and Selected Poems* (Farrar, Straus & Giroux, 2002)

p. 99: "Just When You Think It's Over: A Kind of Grammar Lesson" epigraph is from personal correspondence with Jack Ridl.

p. 103: "The Thing Is" title comes from Ellen Bass's poem "The Thing Is," found in *Poetry of Presence: An Anthology of Mindfulness Poems*, edited by Phyllis Cole-Dai and Ruby R. Wilson (Grayson Books, 2017)

Rosemerry Wahtola Trommer's poetry has appeared in *O Magazine*, TEDx, in back alleys, on *A Prairie Home Companion* and on river rocks she leaves around town. Her poems have been described as "a deep oasis for all who seek to experience the sacred in every moment." Her most recent collection, *Naked for Tea,* was a finalist for the Able Muse Poetry Prize. Other recent books include *Even Now, The Miracle Already Happening* and *The Less I Hold.* She's included in the acclaimed anthology, *Poetry of Presence: An Anthology of Mindfulness Poems,* and leads mindfulness poetry discussion groups.

She served as San Miguel County's first poet laureate and as Western Slope Poet Laureate (2015-2017) and was a finalist for Colorado Poet Laureate (2019). Since 2006, she's written a poem a day. Favorite themes in her poems include parenting, gardening, the natural world, love, thriving/failure and daily life. She's performed and taught poetry for Think 360, Craig Hospital, Ah Haa School for the Arts, Weehawken Arts, Camp Coca Cola, meditation retreats (with Susie Harrington), 12-step recovery programs, hospice, Deepak Chopra, Shyft, and many other organizations.

She is the co-host of Emerging Form, a podcast on creative process (with Christie Aschwanden), co-host of the Talking Gourds Poetry Club (with Art Goodtimes), and co-leader of Secret Agents of Change (with Sherry Richert Belul). Though she earned an MA in English Language & Linguistics at UW-Madison, she still can't effectively pair socks.

Favorite one-word mantra: Adjust.

www.wordwoman.com

Middle Creek Publishing Titles

Fiction

Messiah Complex and Other Stories	Michael Olin-Hitt
Sphinx	Andrea DeJean

Poetry

Span	David Anthony Martin
Deepening the Map	David Anthony Martin
Phases	Erika Moss Gordon
Cirque & Sky	Kathleen Willard
Lessons from Fighting The Black Snake at Standing Rock	Nick Jaina
	Leslie Orihel
Wild Be	One Leaf
Bijoux	David Anthony Martin
Sawhorse	Tony Burfield
Almost Everything, Almost Nothing	KB Ballentine
Kimono Mountain	Mike Parker
p a l e o s	Hoag Holmgren
I	Bengt O Björklund
Across the Light	Bruce Owens
Faces of Fishing Creek	Kyle Laws
a daughter's aubade	Mara Adamitz Scrupe
Secondary Cicatrices	Lynne Goldsmith
Unraveling the Endless Sky	Sandra Noel
The Ground Nest	David Anthony Martin
A Wild Silence	John Noland
The Shaman Speaks	Joseph Murphy
Erodes On Air	Mark Goodwin
Hush	Rosemerry Wahtola Trommer
Catchments	E. A. Lechleitner

Non-Fiction

No Better Place: A New Zen Primer	Hoag Holmgren

About Middle Creek Publishing

MIDDLE CREEK PUBLISHING believes that responding to the world through art & literature — and sharing that response — is a vital part of being an artist.

MIDDLE CREEK PUBLISHING is a company seeking to make the world a better place through both the means and ends of publishing. We are publishers of quality literature in any genre from authors and artists, both seasoned and as-yet undervalued, with a great interest in works which may be considered to be, illuminate or embody any aspect of contemplative Human Ecology, defined as the relationship between humans and their natural, social, and built environments.

MIDDLE CREEK's particular interest in Human Ecology, is meant to clarify an aspect of the quality in the works we will consider for publication, and is meant as a guide to those considering submitting work to us. Our interest is in publishing works illuminating the Human experience through words, story or other content that connects us to each other, our environment, our history and our potential deeply and more consciously.

Made in the USA
Monee, IL
23 September 2023